Full STEAM
Technology Ti...

Robots at Work

Cynthia O'Brien

CRABTREE PUBLISHING COMPANY
WWW.CRABTREEBOOKS.COM

Title-Specific Learning Objectives:

Readers will:
- Define what a robot is and give different examples of robots and the jobs they do.
- Explain why people depend on robots.
- Identify that the main idea is that robots are machines that do work on their own, and retell examples.

High-frequency words (grade one)	Academic vocabulary
a, can, in, is, it, make, on, the, this, too	astronaut, dangerous, information, machine, robot

Before, During, and After Reading Prompts:

Activate Prior Knowledge and Make Predictions:
Create a K-W-L Chart in which children share what they already know, what they would like to know, and what they learned on a subject. Fill in the K and W sections of the chart prior to reading. Look at the title and cover images. Ask children:

- What is a robot?
- What do robots look like?
- What kind of work do robots do?
- Do we use or need robots in our lives? How?
- What would you like to know about robots and the work they do?

During Reading:
After reading pages 6 to 9, ask children to repeat the examples of everyday robots at home and in the community. Review the definition of a robot on page 4: A machine that can do work on its own. Ask children:

- How do the examples of robots fit the definition? What work does each robot do on its own?

After Reading:
Fill in the "L" section of the K-W-L chart. Then, conduct a walk around the room or surrounding area. Have children make a list of robots they see in the community. Talk about how they know each of their choices are robots.

Author: Cynthia O'Brien
Series Development: Reagan Miller
Editor: Janine Deschenes
Proofreader: Melissa Boyce
STEAM Notes for Educators: Janine Deschenes
Guided Reading Leveling: Publishing Solutions Group

Cover, Interior Design, and Prepress: Samara Parent
Photo research: Samara Parent
Production coordinator: Katherine Berti
Photographs:
NASA: p. 17 (both)
Shutterstock: VTT Studio: title page; Borka Kiss: p. 5 (t); Ceri Breeze: p. 8
All other photographs by Shutterstock

Library and Archives Canada Cataloguing in Publication

Title: Robots at work / Cynthia O'Brien.
Names: O'Brien, Cynthia (Cynthia J.), author.
Description: Series statement: Full STEAM ahead! | Includes index.
Identifiers: Canadiana (print) 20190133783 |
 Canadiana (ebook) 20190133791 |
 ISBN 9780778764526 (softcover) |
 ISBN 9780778764069 (hardcover) |
 ISBN 9781427123589 (HTML)
Subjects: LCSH: Robots—Juvenile literature. |
 LCSH: Robots, Industrial—Juvenile literature.
Classification: LCC TJ211.2 .O27 2019 | DDC j629.8/92—dc23

Library of Congress Cataloging-in-Publication Data

Names: O'Brien, Cynthia (Cynthia J.), author.
Title: Robots at work / Cynthia O'Brien.
Description: New York : Crabtree Publishing Company, 2019. |
 Series: Full STEAM ahead! | Includes index.
Identifiers: LCCN 2019023727 (print) | LCCN 2019023728 (ebook) |
 ISBN 9780778764069 (hardcover) |
 ISBN 9780778764526 (paperback) |
 ISBN 9781427123589 (ebook)
Subjects: LCSH: Robots--Juvenile literature. | Robots, Industrial--
 Juvenile literature.
Classification: LCC TJ211.2 .O27 2019 (print) | LCC TJ211.2 (ebook) |
 DDC 629.8/92--dc23
LC record available at https://lccn.loc.gov/2019023727
LC ebook record available at https://lccn.loc.gov/2019023728

Printed in the U.S.A./102019/CG20190809

Table of Contents

What is a Robot? 4

At Home 6

In the Community 8

Again and Again 10

Robot Builders 12

Making Things 14

Dangerous Jobs 16

Keeping Safe 18

Future Robots 20

Words to Know 22

Index and About the Author 23

Crabtree Plus Digital Code 23

STEAM Notes for Educators 24

Crabtree Publishing Company
www.crabtreebooks.com   1-800-387-7650

Copyright © **2020 CRABTREE PUBLISHING COMPANY**. All rights reserved. No part of this publication may be reproduced, stored in a retrieval system or be transmitted in any form or by any means, electronic, mechanical, photocopying, recording, or otherwise, without the prior written permission of Crabtree Publishing Company. In Canada: We acknowledge the financial support of the Government of Canada through the Book Publishing Industry Development Program (BPIDP) for our publishing activities.

Published in Canada
Crabtree Publishing
616 Welland Ave.
St. Catharines, Ontario
L2M 5V6

Published in the United States
Crabtree Publishing
PMB 59051
350 Fifth Avenue, 59th Floor
New York, New York 10118

Published in the United Kingdom
Crabtree Publishing
Maritime House
Basin Road North, Hove
BN41 1WR

Published in Australia
Crabtree Publishing
Unit 3 – 5 Currumbin Court
Capalaba
QLD 4157

What is a Robot?

A robot is a **machine** that can do work on its own. Robots make jobs easier, safer, and more fun.

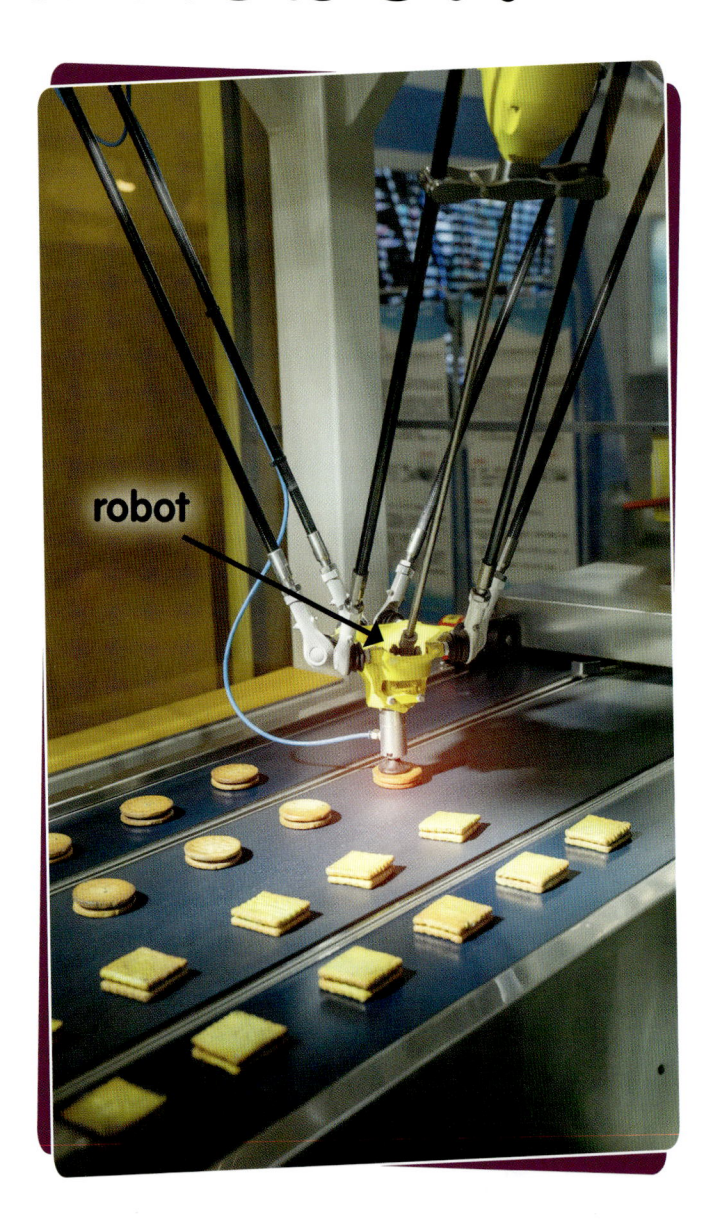

robot

This robot makes tasty cookies!

robot

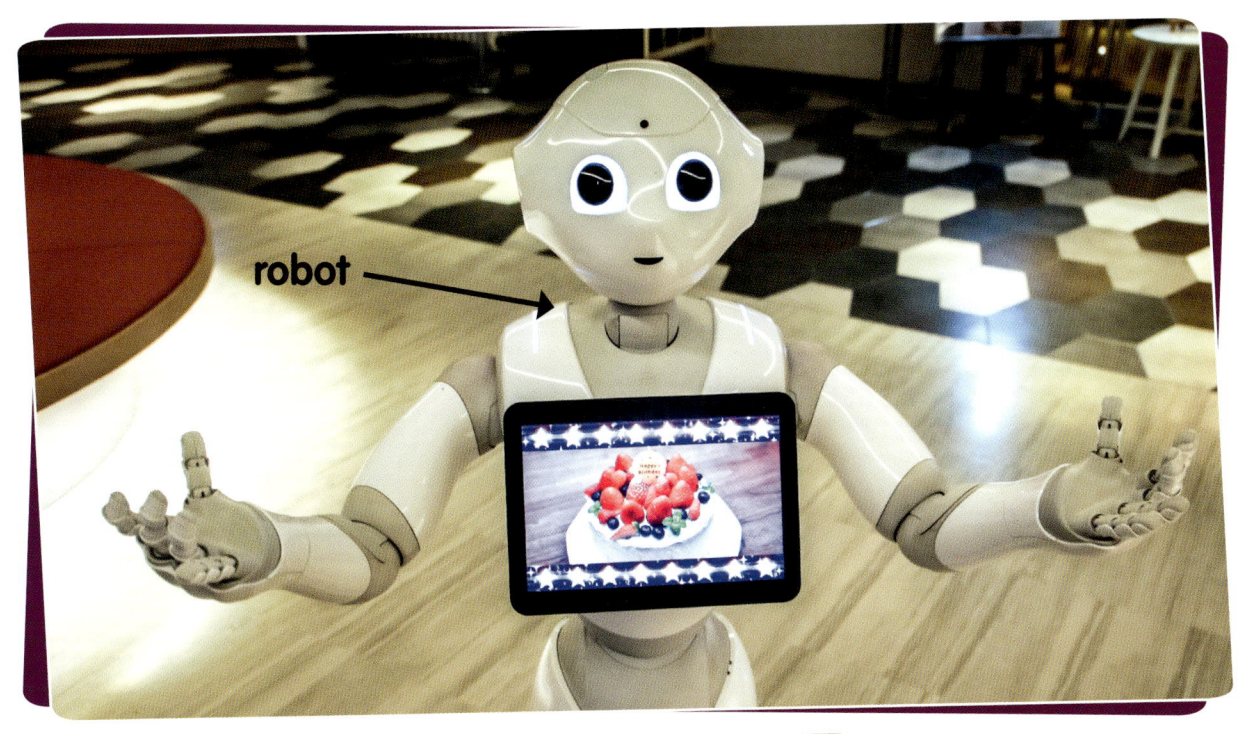

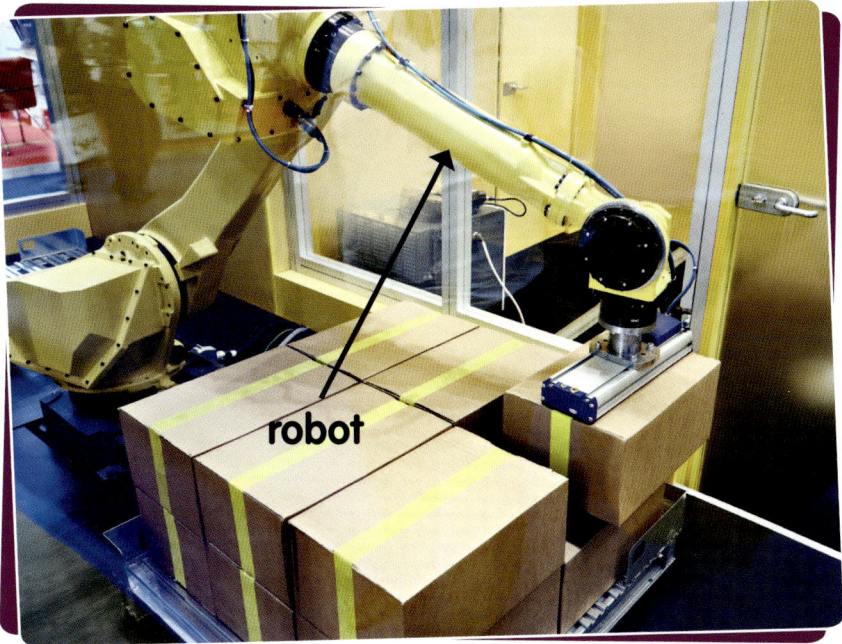

This robot can talk and give **information** on a screen.

robot

This is a robot too. It packs boxes.

5

At Home

Robots help us every day. They do jobs inside and outside our homes.

robot

This robot understands voices that tell it what to do. It can find information on the Internet, play music, and turn on the lights.

This robot can clean the pool.

It is easy to cut the grass with this robot!

In the Community

Robots are all around us. Can you find robots in your community?

This train is a robot! It moves up and down the **track** without a driver.

A bank machine counts out the money that you need.

The brushes and hoses in a car wash can clean your car on their own.

9

Again and Again

A robot can do the same job again and again. It never gets tired!

This robot picks up and moves packages so they can be mailed to people. It makes the same movements all day.

This robot fills empty bottles with water. It fills the bottles with the same amount of water every time.

11

Robot Builders

People use robots to build things. Robots can make building jobs faster and safer.

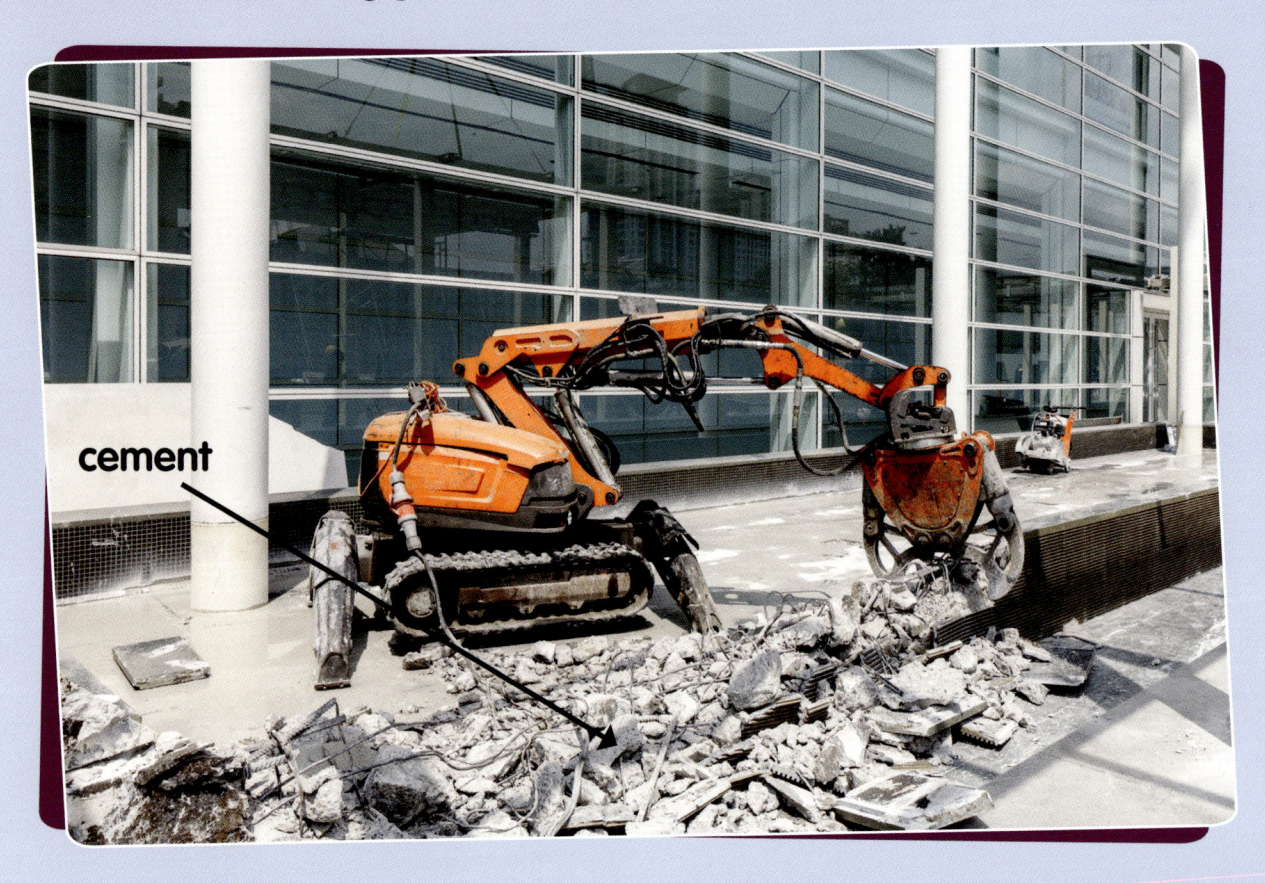

cement

Robots that build can be very strong. This robot breaks through thick cement.

steel beam

This robot uses heat and power to join steel beams. These are long, strong bars that are used in buildings. This job can hurt people, but robots can do it safely.

13

Making Things

Some machines have many parts. Robots help to put the parts together.

People give this robot **instructions** on a computer. The instructions tell the robot how to put parts together.

All of these cars need the same parts. Robots put the parts together. They do this job over and over. They put the parts together the same way every time.

Dangerous Jobs

Robots can do jobs that are too dangerous for people. Something that is dangerous can cause harm.

Working deep underwater can be dangerous for humans. So this robot does the job! It takes pictures of what it finds.

Working in space is dangerous! **Astronauts** use robots to help them.

robot

This robot astronaut does jobs that are difficult or unsafe for people. For example, it uses **delicate** tools.

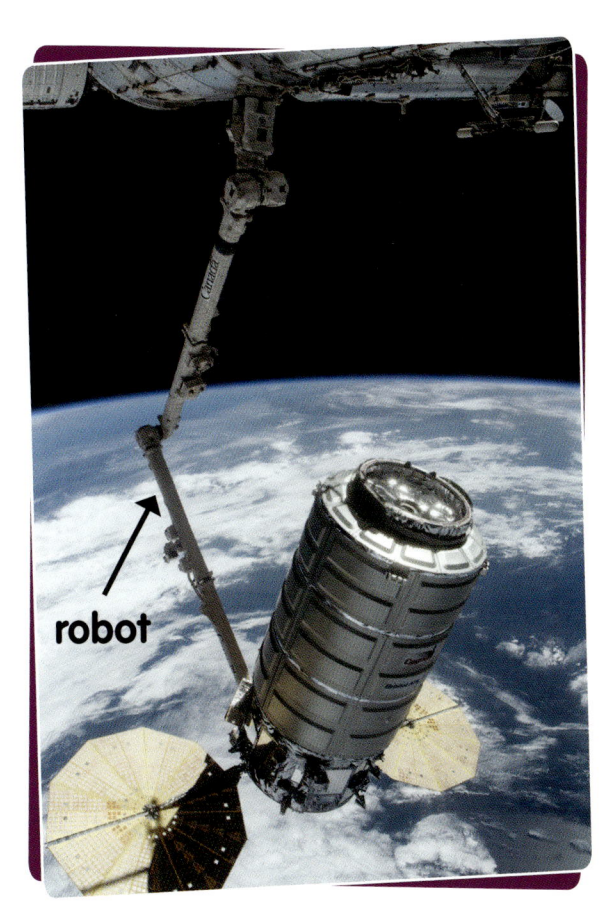

This robot can do dangerous or difficult repairs in space.

17

Keeping Safe

Robots help to keep us safe. They **protect** us from danger. They can also help people do dangerous jobs more safely.

Some firefighters use robots to help them fight fire. This robot takes a video of a wildfire. The video lets firefighters see exactly where the fire is.

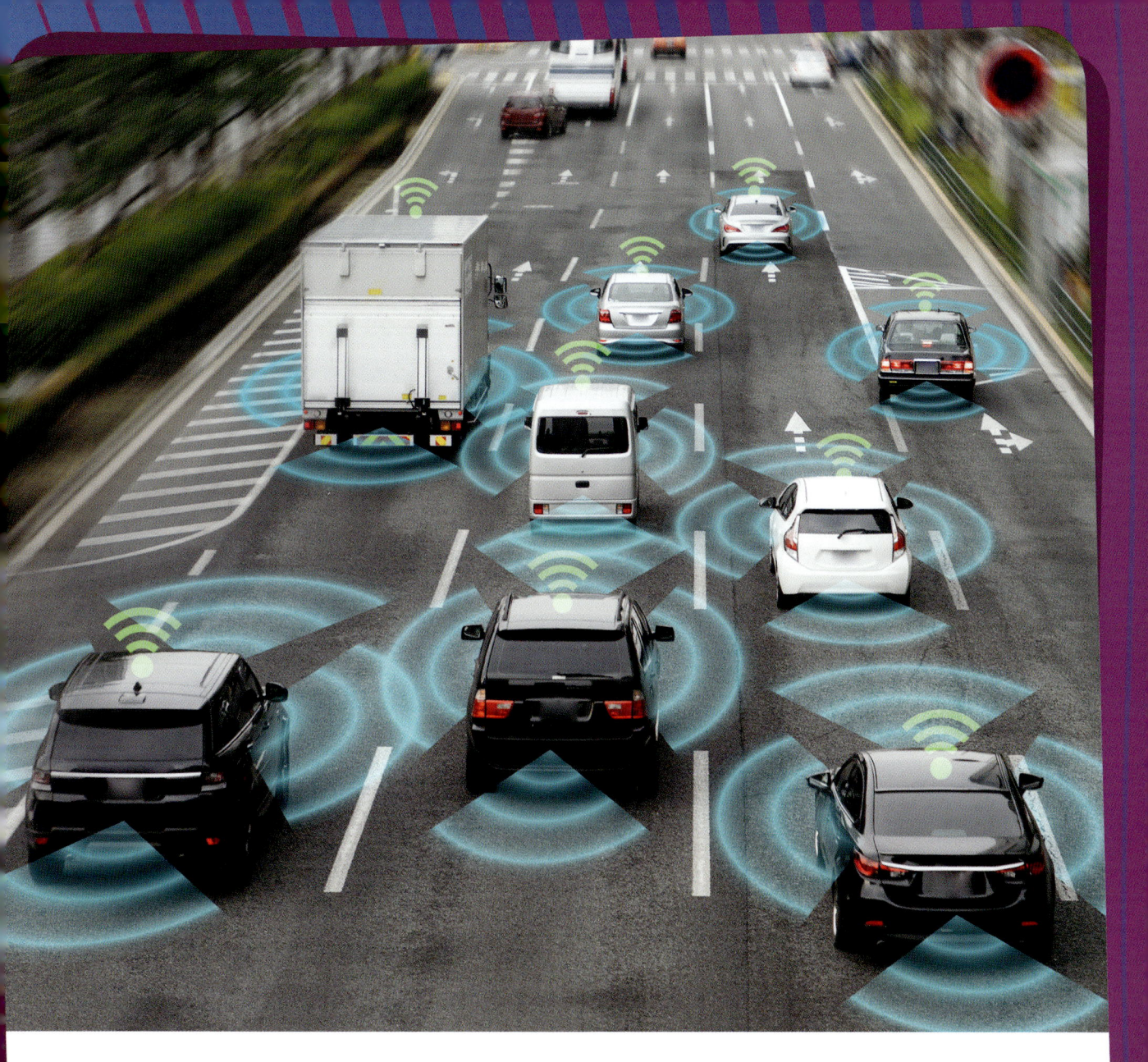

Some cars have robot parts. The parts do safety jobs such as making sure the car does not hit objects around it. They work on their own to help keep people safe!

Future Robots

People **invent** robots all the time. Would you like to make a robot? What jobs would your robot do?

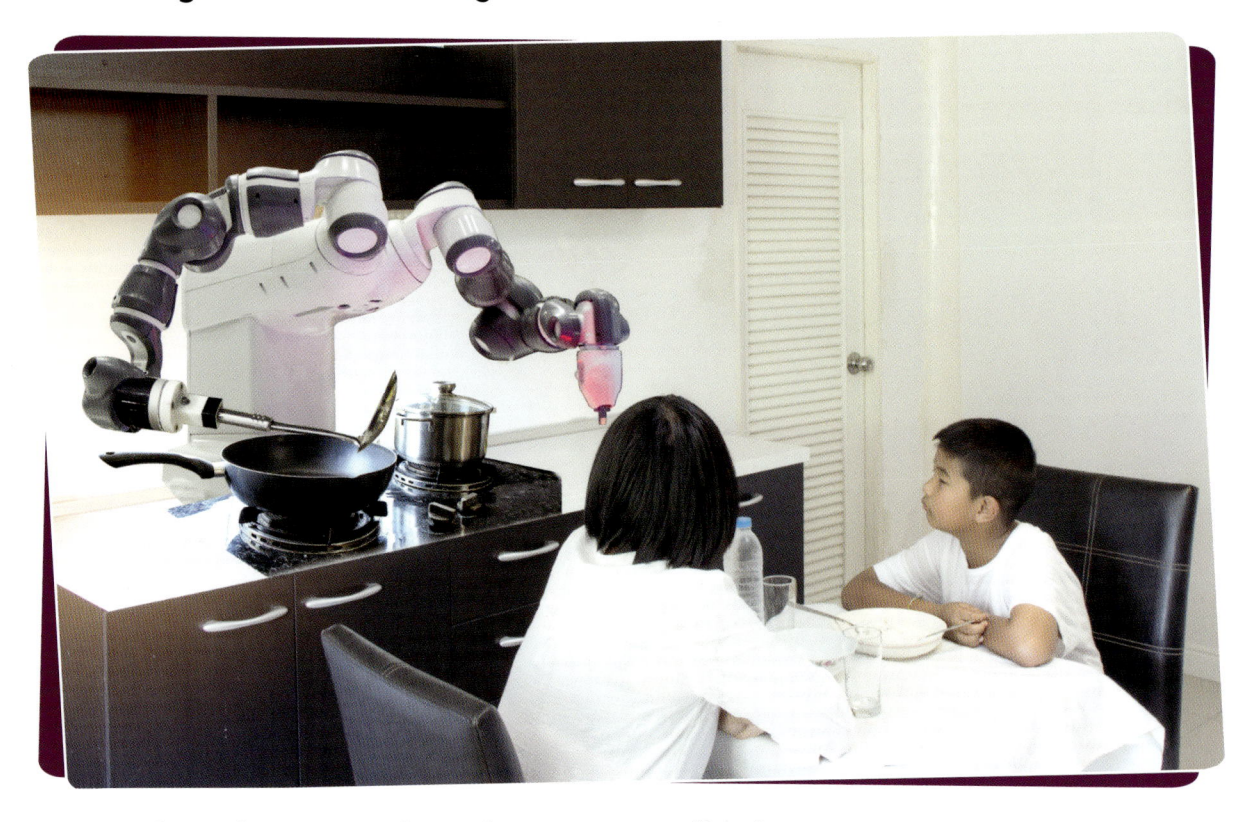

One day, there may be robots in your kitchen! Would you like a robot to make your dinner?

A delivery robot could bring your shopping to your home. Some people are already working on building these robots!

A robot may go to the store for you.

Words to Know

astronaut [AS-tr*uh*-nawt] noun Person whose job it is to travel into outer space

delicate [DEL-i-kit] adjective Easily broken; needs careful handling

information [in-fer-MEY-sh*uh*n] noun Knowledge passed on

instructions [in-STRUHK-sh*uh*ns] noun A set of steps that tells us how to do something

invent [in-VENT] verb To create something new

machine [muh-SHEEN] noun A tool with one or more parts used to do work

protect [pruh-TEKT] verb To keep from being hurt

track [trak] noun The structure along which a train moves

A noun is a person, place, or thing.
A verb is an action word that tells you what someone or something does.
An adjective is a word that tells you what something is like.

Index

bank machine 9
cars 9, 15, 19
firefighters 18
home 6–7, 20–21
parts 14–15, 19

safety 12–13, 16–19
shopping 21
space 17
train 8
underwater 16

About the Author

Cynthia O'Brien has written many books for young readers. It is fun to help make a technology like a book! Books can be full of stories. They also teach you about the world around you, including other technologies—like robots.

To explore and learn more, enter the code at the Crabtree Plus website below.

www.crabtreeplus.com/fullsteamahead

Your code is:
fsa20

STEAM Notes for Educators

Full STEAM Ahead is a literacy series that helps readers build vocabulary, fluency, and comprehension while learning about big ideas in STEAM subjects. *Robots at Work* helps readers identify the main idea of the book and give examples of robots that support the main idea. The STEAM activity below helps readers extend the ideas in the book to build their skills in technology and engineering.

Activity title

Children will be able to:
- Understand that a robot is a machine that can do work on its own, and sort types of robots based on whether they help make life easier, safer, or more fun.
- Create a plan for a robot that makes life easier, safer, or more fun.

Materials
- Sorting Robots Worksheet
- Pictures or videos of various robots at work
- Robot Plan Worksheet

Guiding Prompts
After reading *Robots at Work*, ask children:
- What is a robot?
- What are some jobs that robots do?
- Why do humans use robots to do jobs?
- Can you think of any robots in your community?

Activity Prompts
Tell children that they will explore different kinds of robots—and make a plan to create their own! First, hand each child a Sorting Robots Worksheet. Then, show children pictures or videos of various robots at work. Read and display the type of robot as well. You can use examples from the book, and other outside examples. Each time a picture is shown, the child should write down the type of robot on the chart. They will sort the robots by whether they make life easier, safer, or more fun. When the activity is complete, talk to the children about how they sorted the robots.
Do any robots fit into more than one column? Did you have difficulty sorting any robots?

Tell children that they will make their own plan for a robot that makes life easier, safer, or more fun. They will use the Robot Plan Worksheet to draw and explain their robot. Display the finished worksheets.

Extensions
- Connect with computational thinking by having children "program" their robots to do their jobs. Have them write instructions for the robot to follow. Work in pairs to read the instructions and check whether they will correctly instruct the robot to do its job. Make improvements and present instructions.

To view and download the worksheets, visit **www.crabtreebooks.com/resources/printables** or **www.crabtreeplus.com/fullsteamahead** and enter the code **fsa20**.